ALL IS FAIR IN LOVE AND SALES

All is Fair in Love and Sales;

Six Steps to Sales Success

By Chris Singleton

ALL IS FAIR IN LOVE AND SALES

Copyright Page

All rights reserved. No part of this publication may be reproduced or transmitted in any form or by any means, electronic or mechanical, including photocopying, recording, or any other information storage and retrieval system, without the written permission of the publisher.

For permission requests, write to the publisher, addressed "Attention: Permissions Coordinator," at the address below.
Allisfairinloveandsales@gmail.com

Ordering information
Quantity Sales. Special discounts are available on quantity purchases by corporations, associations, or networking groups.
Includes biographical references and index

ALL IS FAIR IN LOVE AND SALES

ALL IS FAIR IN LOVE AND SALES

Foreword:

Hi, my name is ***Johnny "Macknificent Mack"***. In 2001, I was the World's #1 Salesperson for Mitsubishi Motors. I went on to become the second-place winner in their National Walk Around Contest. I share this with you to provide context as to why I can evaluate this awesome book presented by Mr. Chris Singleton.

I met Chris at a networking event, and as usual he was networking. He stood out in this crowded venue for two reasons. Number one, he was poised and possessed an air of confidence and conviction. Number two, I was struck that at his young age he displayed these attributes.

I made it a point to meet with Mr. Singleton and get his contact information. We had an enlightening and powerful phone connection about a week later and I discovered just how remarkable Chris is. At a tender young age, he began studying the craft of sales and implemented his findings into a lucrative automobile sales career! He then parlayed that expertise into owning his own sales training, coaching and consulting business. Here Chris worked with fortune 500 clients training sales professionals, management and leaders all over the world in all genres of business from automotive sales to mortgage lending, to financial services to insurance to media sales and virtually everything in between!

Mr. Singleton has worked with and trained some of the top sales and leadership professionals in the country and brings a wealth of knowledge in this arena. Yet it is not that impressive background that captured my attention (although it did), rather it was his attention to detail and understanding of the craft that made me realize that Chris is indeed a giant among men.

There are many people that possess the gift of sales, yet they are unable to transfer that information in a meaningful manner. Chris has developed the skillset to present his knowledge at a cellular level. This book is just the starting point of an information transformation that will surely lift all who partake to new levels of success and significance.

ALL IS FAIR IN LOVE AND SALES

I highly recommend this book to anyone in sales, business, entrepreneurship, aspiring entrepreneurship and any professionals that want to become better. To those that are leading their companies and fields, I endorse this book to help you become the best. Further, if you get the opportunity to see Chris Singleton speak or present live…GO!

Johnny "Macknificent" Mack
The WRITE Coach

ALL IS FAIR IN LOVE AND SALES

Table of Contents

Contents

Foreword:	5
Table of Contents	8
Dedication	9
Intro:	13
What to expect from this book	21
Chapter 1: Effective Introductions	23
Chapter 2: Presentations: Best practices	41
Chapter 3: Closing	55
Chapter 4: Objection Handling	87
Chapter 5: Referrals	103
Chapter 6: Follow up	117
Afterword	125
About the Author	126

ALL IS FAIR IN LOVE AND SALES

Dedication

This book is dedicated first and foremost to my son Christopher Amari Singleton. The moment that I became aware of your existence you inspired change in me. You inspire me to be better each day!

I also want to dedicate this to a few people who helped me along the way.

The Bowers family- You all taught me valuable lessons in loyalty, love and forgiveness that I will never forget.

Cyntia Hightower(and family)- You showed me love and made me feel like I was one of your sons. I will forever be grateful.

Ann Canton(aka "Momma Ann")- Your kindness and generosity will never be forgotten! Thank you for help along the way!

Vance Bailey- My first sales manager. You taught me valuable life lessons in my transition from a boy to a man.

Trenton Boe- You are the definition of character personified. Thank you for your guidance.

ALL IS FAIR IN LOVE AND SALES

Mark Wimberly- You always encouraged me to think outside of the box and helped me to see possibilities beyond the immediate.

Eric Winchester- You taught me so many lessons in sales that I will never forget.

Trevor Watkins- You encouraged me always!

Center Texas Teachers- Vicki Edge, Betsy Porter, Angela Koonce, Tarska Duffield, Tresa Konderla, Joyce Biggers- Linda Snell. You all had reach that extended well beyond the classroom and all touched my life in a different and positive!

ALL IS FAIR IN LOVE AND SALES

ALL IS FAIR IN LOVE AND SALES

ALL IS FAIR IN LOVE AND SALES

Intro:

My love affair with sales began when I was a mere child living in the small rural town of Center, Texas. At only 8 years old, I began to learn about sales, supply, demand and how to use these dynamics to my advantage.

Due to my parents earning just above the poverty line, I qualified for "free" lunch at the elementary school cafeteria. This lunch usually consisted of lukewarm food, a stale dessert and your choice of chocolate or regular milk.

One day while I was in the free lunch line, I noticed a new kid. We began chatting and he stated that his name was John and he had just been transferred to my elementary school because his dad moved here on business. As we approached the lunch checkout where you either show your lunch card or say your last name, I proceeded with checkout, and then observed that John was having trouble checking out. After a few seconds, I heard the lunch lady bellow, "I'm sorry, little John, but you are not on the free lunch program.

The pay lunch line is over there." I watched as John walked over to the pay lunch line with a look of dejection in his eyes. He ordered his lunch along with an orange juice and sat down alone.

I wasn't very popular myself, so I walked over to him, sat down across the table and said, "What's wrong? Your food is much better than the food that we get in the free lunch line. Why would you want to eat in the free lunch line?"

"Milk." He stated. I don't really like orange juice. I prefer milk, but it is only available in the free lunch line. I looked at his orange juice and thought, "I am so tired of milk... I would love to have his orange juice." So, I suggested that we trade. My milk for his orange juice. This went on for a couple of days until one day I asked John. "How much are you paying for these orange juices?" "$2.25," he stated. "Wow," I thought. "That is enough to buy so much candy!" So, I told John that instead of buying me the orange juice, why doesn't he just pay me the $2.25? "No biggie," he stated.

ALL IS FAIR IN LOVE AND SALES

Around that time, I noticed multiple food trays with unopened or barely opened milk cartons. "If only these kids knew that because milk isn't available in the pay lunch line that their milk could be worth something," I thought. So, I decided to try an experiment.

The next day as soon as the bell sounded signifying lunch time, I raced down to the cafeteria and ate my lunch quickly. I then went around and asked all the kids who had not yet opened their milk cartons if they were going to drink their milk and if not, then would they mind if I had it? For the kids that needed a little extra incentive, I would offer to give them 25 cents. In my mind, .25 cents was a small price to pay to make $2.25. Before I knew it I had collected 9 cartons of milk with the intention of selling them all for $2.25.

One big mistake that I made was that I didn't take into consideration the fact that I only knew 1 kid who preferred milk over orange juice and the other soft drinks available in the paid lunch line and would pay $2.25 for the milk. I went around to other children who were in the paid lunch line to see who was interested in purchasing one of my pints of milk for $2.25.

Needless to say, the response was abysmal. "Are you crazy?" One student said. After lunch, the rest of the day just seemed to drag on. I felt rejected, and worst of all I had spent the entire $2.25 that I obtained from John that day on purchasing other children's milk for 25 cents a piece. I remember getting off the bus that day and walking into my room and throwing my backpack full of milk against the wall in frustration.

The next morning in science class, Mrs. Koonce was discussing the subject of bones.

"In order for bones to be healthy, they need calcium. Milk contains more calcium than virtually any drink that you can drink." She concluded... "So kids, think twice before drinking all of those sugary sodas and remember if you want strong bones, what do you need to drink?" "MILK!!!!" the whole class shouted in unison.

ALL IS FAIR IN LOVE AND SALES

Directly afterwards, the lunch bell rang and despite my misfortune the day before, I ran down to the cafeteria with a backpack full of the milk from the previous day and a renewed sense of confidence. The response was totally different!

The same kids who declined offers before to purchase milk from me were now purchasing it from me without a second thought. Not because it tasted any different but because Mrs. Koonce had now created a demand for milk after teaching a class and citing its health benefits. Halfway through lunch, I had already nearly sold out all my pints of milk, and with only 1 more left, I approached my final table.

"This is my last milk," I stated. "I'll take it," said Zach. "No, I'll take it," said Mark. "I'll pay $2.50 for it," said Zach. "Well, I'll pay $2.75 for it," said Mark. This went on for a little while until Mark won the bidding at $3.50. I made a total of $22 in just 1 lunch period!

The supply of milk was low at least to the kids who weren't on the free lunch program because milk wasn't available to them. The demand was high due to the recent science class that Mrs. Koonce conducted regarding bones and the effects of calcium on those bones and the fact that milk is high in calcium. This sudden but dramatic paradigm shift in the minds of those students at Center Elementary school sparked my lifelong obsession and fascination with this phenomenon called sales!

ALL IS FAIR IN LOVE AND SALES

ALL IS FAIR IN LOVE AND SALES

ALL IS FAIR IN LOVE AND SALES

What to expect from this book

In this book, you will learn the 6 steps to successful selling and how to master them. Consider this your step by step guide to sales and influence. If you can learn to master these 6 steps to successful selling, you will not only make more money, but also be an overall more persuasive individual.

The contents contained inside will truly transcend your life if you put the things that you will learn into practice. It may alter how you negotiate for cars or homes. How you communicate with your friends or spouses, how you interview for jobs or make first impressions on the various people that you will meet throughout your life. Most importantly, however, the contents inside will help you to harness arguably life's most essential skill...Sales! To enter this truly transcendent experience, turn to the next page!

ALL IS FAIR IN LOVE AND SALES

Chapter 1: Effective Introductions

An argument can be made as to which one of these keys to successful selling is the most important; however, few stronger arguments can be made than the introduction. This is where the sale begins! Before we dive into introductions. First, let's take a look at first impressions. This is important because many people don't realize just how important the first impression is, why it is so important, nor how it sets the tone not only for the introduction, but for the entire sales process as well.

The Science of First Impressions

According to one Yale University study, a first impression can be formulated in as little as 1/10th of a second, and if given another 5 seconds to formulate a first impression 91% of the time the first impression stayed the exact same as it was during the first 1/10th of a second. How does this happen so fast? Why does this first impression stay the same even when given more time to formulate? How can you make a great first impression?

First, let's look at why and how this happens so fast. The human brain uses something called heuristics or the brain's subconscious "rules of thumb" based on previous experiences. As humans, we are faced with hundreds of decisions each day. So, the brain compensates for this by using heuristics to make snap decisions and assumptions based on previous experiences and the immediate data that is received during the initial encounter with a person, place or thing.

For example; when walking down the street, if we see a piano hanging from a rope above the sidewalk, most of us wouldn't have to stop and calculate the probability of it falling on our heads. Most of us would simply walk around that piano "instinctively" and probably without even breaking stride. This is because of heuristics which many people equate to intuition or instincts. The brain uses these "mental shortcuts" to predict or presume potential outcomes or to avoid risks. As studies show, this happens almost immediately.

First impressions usually don't change. In fact, 91% of the time they stay the same from the first 1/10th of a second onward. Why? Well, this is because of a cognitive bias called confirmation bias. Simply put, whatever our initial impression or "bias" of someone is, the brain automatically tries to provide supporting data to confirm what that initial bias was.

For instance, if a person decides that you're a jerk as their first impression then the brain will likely start to send confirmations such as, "He also has a bald head... and my uncle whom I don't like has a bald head also" or "she has freckles... the girl that broke my heart in high school had freckles" and so on and so forth. The inverse can also be said regarding a positive first impression. So, first impressions can shape the sale or set the tone for our entire interaction with someone more than we may realize.

Making a Positive First Impression:
Since the first impression happens so fast and often before we can even open our mouths, is it even possible to make a great first impression? Well, obviously, the answer

to that is yes! In fact, there are five primary deciding factors in an in-person first impression of you. This is, of course, speaking about an in-person first impression.

1. **Eye Contact-** Two key attributes that most consumers look out for before deciding on a product or service is confidence and trustworthiness. If you are looking someone in the eyes and making good solid continuous eye contact with such person, studies show that most people perceive that as a sign of both confidence and trustworthiness.
2. **Dress-** This doesn't mean that you have to have the most expensive garb. However, things such as properly hemmed slacks, a pressed shirt, and if what you are selling causes for a full suit, then having a properly fitting suit, fewer wrinkles the better and have shoes that are in decent condition, all can have an effect on a first impression. For women, the same is true, business length skirts/ dresses and modest cuts can help to ensure that the consumer sees beyond your attire. Dress can often be viewed as a physical representation of a person's work ethic or

attention to detail. One poll states that 94% of the time, the first thing that a person notices when formulating the first impression is dress. Important? I think so!

3. **Grooming-** One survey says that when shown a picture of 2 men... one with facial hair and the other clean-shaven. 72% of the time, the surveyors said the one with the clean-shaven face appeared more trustworthy. Intermediate studies were also conducted, and those studies also supported the connection between less facial hair and appearing more trustworthy. Before the guys who wear goatees or other forms of facial hair close this book, I am not saying that you must go clean shaven or you will not be successful. I am simply suggesting that if you can go without it then it may serve you well. For women, a similar study was conducted regarding bangs that covered a part of the face and with similar results. The less hair in the face the more trustworthy they were perceived by others. Many psychologists believe that this is due to the brain equating openness

of the face to transparency, honesty or "openness" of someone's character.

4. **Body Language**- Many independent studies show that over 70% of communication is nonverbal or "body language". Some studies even go as far as to say that nonverbal communication accounts for up to 93% of all communication. Whether it is 70%, 93% or somewhere in between, I think that we can all agree that it is very important. So here are a few tips for ensuring that your body language is positive.

- Smile- Even if you have had a bad day, few things make people feel more at ease than a warm smile
- Show Extremities- When hands are hiding in pockets, it often can give the perception that you have something else to hide or there is something else that you are not being honest about or won't be honest about in the future.
- Face your prospect- The direction that your body faces is often a good indicator of where you want to go. For instance, at the end of a meeting, you may notice someone place their

feet in a direction that is pointing toward the door, and then leave shortly thereafter. This happens subconsciously... because you face the direction that you want to go... not facing a prospect can show signs of **disinterest**.

5. **Tonality and Pace-** Don't underestimate the importance of tonality and pace when speaking, especially during the first impression. Speaking in an authoritative or condescending tone can indicate arrogance or aggression and speaking in a timid or an apologetic tone could give the perception of a lack of confidence and unsureness. Likewise, speaking with too fast of a pace can give the perception of "slickness" or deceit, while speaking at too slow of a pace can give the perception of a lack of confidence and/or incompetence. So be mindful of your tonality and pace! Speaking at a moderate pace, altering between vocal quadrants and allowing your voice inflection to reflect confidence in your product or service is key.

ALL IS FAIR IN LOVE AND SALES

Pique Interest

There are two things that are imperative to do during an introduction. The first thing is to pique interest and the second thing is to establish intent.

"Sir, I have pudding in my pants but that is not why I'm here!" This was literally the introductory statement made to me by a door to door salesman by the name of Mark who came knocking on my door one Tuesday evening. Our introductory dialogue went a little something like this:

Mark: Hello Sir, I have pudding in my pants but that's not why I'm here.
Me: Excuse me?
Mark: I said I have pudding in my pants but that's not why I'm here.
Me: O….k…. Why are you here then?
Mark: I'm glad that you asked… I will continue. I am here because I was just over there speaking with your neighbors regarding these magazines for our fundraiser…etc.
Me: I laughed and said: "I will take it." Whatever you are selling, I will take it.

Now, I am by no means encouraging this introduction as a standard practice. I will say, however, the way he grabbed my attention or piqued my interest at the beginning has been unparalleled by anything that I have seen since.

Likewise, an introduction should be something that engages the listener. Three of the most effective ways to do this are below. Depending on what you're selling, one of the methods or perhaps multiple of these methods could be appropriate:

1. Pose a thought-provoking question. There are two primary types of thought-provoking questions used in an introduction. The first is intrinsic questioning and the second is extrinsic questioning.

Intrinsic questioning is posing a question about the prospect's internal business. Intrinsic introductory questioning is often used when the prospect already has a solution that has a similar function to the solution that you are selling; however, you just want to illustrate how yours is better. This question can often be rhetorical.

A software salesperson may ask, "How much money is your current solution really costing you in revenue each quarter?" Or "Are you really capturing as many customers from your database as you could be?"

Intrinsic questioning is questioning that is often followed by illustrating a current deficiency in the prospect's current product or service (without bashing their current provider), discussing how that may be affecting their business (costs, time, customer retention...etc.) followed by how your product or service will be just what the doctor ordered.

Extrinsic questioning is posing a question about how the prospect's business would be affected if it had a particular solution. This type of introductory questioning is often used for prospects who don't have a similar solution to your particular product or service.

A software salesperson may ask, "If you could automate X, Y and Z tasks, how much money and time would that save you as an organization?" An automobile salesperson may ask... "How much more convenient would it be if you had a 3rd row vehicle to accommodate your growing family?"

This type of questioning is often followed by a story of a prospect who didn't have this product or service previously but now that they have it, it has changed the landscape of their business. Or it may be followed by painting a picture of how the prospect's business would look with the addition of this product or service. How much more efficient operations would be, how much more the customers would be satisfied, and/or how much more revenue would be created.

This method is effective because when used properly it can cause a prospect to look at their business differently. It will often cause the prospect to re-think their current solution or to think about the business that they aren't obtaining due to not having a solution with the capabilities that your solution has.

2. Make a bold statement.

In my years of sales training, one of my previous students became a life insurance agent. He utilized this "Make a Bold Statement" method by starting each consultation off with this statement. "You have 24 hours left to live." (Then he paused for a while to let that sink in). He then proceeds to say "Death doesn't give us a 24-hour notice such as the one that I just mentioned. So, the only thing that we can do is prepare." He then commended the prospect for not waiting on the "24-hour notice" and taking action now. He then went into his presentation about if his first statement was true, then how would their family currently be affected? Who would have to cough up the money for the funeral cost? How much money would be left over for the children? How much debt would be left for the family to pay...etc.? Do you think that opening statement captured the prospect's attention? Most definitely!

A bold statement can also be an astonishing fact. I was working with a salesperson who was selling a bi-weekly payment solution to automotive dealers and her introduction was, "According to the American Financial Institute, 70% of

ALL IS FAIR IN LOVE AND SALES

Americans live paycheck to paycheck." This made it obvious that the fact that automobile payments were usually made once a month perhaps wasn't the best.

This method requires finesse because the initial reaction to the statement may be that of shock, surprise, anger or fear. The intention of making a bold statement at the outset of your introduction is to pique the prospect's interest and evoke strong emotion in your prospect from the beginning.

Depending on the gravity of the initial bold statement, it may be important to soothe your client shortly after the impact of your initial statement is felt. You may do this by making a "release statement." A release statement simply lets the prospect off the hook, or "releases" them from the initial emotional impact of the statement. Some examples of release statements are: "What if that were true?" or "Wouldn't it be nice if that were the case?"

This method is often very effective if used properly because it engages the prospect immediately and evokes emotion. You will have the prospect's attention for at least the following moments. Now, all you have to do is keep it!

3. Tell a story that has the 3 Rs; Relevant, Relatable, and Real.

One of my favorite short stories to tell when I was speaking to a group about my sales training and coaching services or when I was doing an inspirational speech was a brief inspirational story involving Helen Keller.

Helen Keller contracted what was then known as Scarlet Fever when she was less than 2 years old. This made her both deaf and blind before her 3rd birthdate; however, she adapted. She learned to sense who walked in the room by how strong the vibrations of their footsteps were. She learned to speak by placing her hands on the lips of her teacher and mimicking the movements of her teacher's lips.

She was the first deaf-blind person to receive a Bachelor of Arts degree. She was also an author, she wrote 12 books. She was elected to the National Women's Hall of Fame. She was also awarded the Presidential Medal of

Freedom. When being interviewed, she was asked a question. "Helen, it must be the worst thing in the world to go through life without sight. Can you think of anything worse?" Her response was, "The only thing worse than being blind is having sight but no vision."

This raises 2 questions. The first question is what is your excuse? The second is, do you have vision?

I then began to speak about perseverance, the importance of having a crystal-clear vision and also how my sales coaching and training program would bring these visions and goals to life. I could literally see the look of empowerment brush over the faces of the audience. This brief story often encouraged the crowd to think about what they wanted out of life and how they could attain those things. This powerful story often opened the minds and the hearts of the listener.

This story is real, relatable and relevant to the product that I was selling. A story embedded in an introduction can be humorous, inspirational, or an impact story. This method is effective because it can humanize you if you are using a personal story. It can inspire change if you are using a story about how your product or service helped a client and lastly, there are few things that get ingrained in a prospect's memory long after you leave like a good short story does!

ALL IS FAIR IN LOVE AND SALES

ALL IS FAIR IN LOVE AND SALES

Chapter 2: Presentations: Best practices

How to Present Anything to Anybody

A presentation is only as effective as your introduction, the questions that you ask prior to the presentation, and if applicable, the research that you have completed on your prospect prior to the presentation. If you don't ask the right questions and probe for a customer or client's needs first, then chances are your presentation is going to fall on deaf ears. A good presentation can have many components; however, one surefire way to ensure that you have a powerful presentation is to remember the **4 Ps** and the **3 Ts**.

The **4 Ps** according to Mike Delconte on the Social Influence Podcast are as follows:
- The first **P** stands for **Promise**. This promise is often delivered in the introduction of your presentation. This often gives a promise as to what your product or service will do. For example, you may tell a customer, "In this presentation, you're going to learn why the

Kia Optima was ranked highest in initial quality out of all vehicles." Or you may say, "You are going to learn why our software company was rated the top according to DeLoitte magazine." This promise is usually a powerful statement or promise of what the customer or consumer is to get if they purchase your product or service.

- This next **P** stands for **Picture**. Picture, you want to paint the picture. A real estate agent may tell a potential customer, "Imagine if, in 30 days, you're walking into your dream home. You were able to have your family and friends over barbecuing in the backyard, and the best part is that you were able to do this fast and efficiently."

Or an automobile salesperson may say, "Picture it, imagine you're driving in a Camry and you see something on the side of the road and you swerve. However, because it has the electronic brake force distribution, even though you swerved, that is still going to keep the vehicle from spinning out of control. Safety is one of the things that really sets the Toyota Camry apart." You want to paint the picture of being able to use your product and service and why it's going to benefit them.

- The next **P** stands for **Proof**. The proof often involves a relevant story that is a proof of your promise. It could also be a third-party statistic or award. However, often time, it is a story...An example of that would be, an automobile salesman may say that Mrs. Johnson purchased the Camry last year, and initially, she wasn't so sure about all the fuel economy claims and the reliability claims, however, she's actually averaging 2.7 miles per gallon over what is estimated on the sticker. That's one of the reasons why, as I mentioned earlier, the Camry is noted the most fuel-efficient passenger sedan in its class.

- The last **P** stands for **Pitch**. This is really the sales portion of your presentation. This is where you're bringing out features and benefits of your particular product or service. When pitching your particular product or service, it's important to remember the **3Ts.**

1. The first **T** stands for, **Tailor your presentation**. There's an adage that says that people don't care how much you know until they know how much you care. Tailoring your presentation to the consumer, shows care and consideration to them. One may do this by illustrating the hot points that the consumer mentioned were important to them earlier. For instance, if a mortgage loan officer was talking to a potential buyer, and the buyer mentioned that what was most important to them when using a loan officer

was that the person was communicative and really communicated with them often and that the person had great customer service, this means that even though the loan process can be an arduous process, that they were patient with the customer.

Then in tailoring that presentation, that loan officer, or that mortgage officer, is going to mention those things and is going to really key in on those two parts of his presentation. He may say, "One of the biggest reasons why people do business with us here at XYZ Mortgage, is because we actually communicate with our customers, we have a follow-up system to always keep our customer in the loop. We actually have an ad that says, 'No customer left behind.' We're extremely patient here, and that's why we have so many second-chance buying programs. Because we know that sometimes in life bad things happen to good people. Our objective is to really be able to help every customer that we can."

When you tailor your presentation to the consumer, it not only makes the customer feel heard and cared about, but it also increases your chances of selling that particular product or service. Many people liken it to when you tell a doctor what your symptoms are. Think of yourself as a doctor in your business. If you're in automobile sales, a doctor of autoology. If you're a mortgage lender, a doctor of loanology. If you're in real estate, a real estate doctor.

When you go to a doctor, you tell a doctor your symptoms and he makes a prescription based on what your symptoms are. Again, it is imperative to conduct a proper needs assessment and to be sure that you have a proper introduction and questioning before the presentation, so that way you can really tailor your presentation and write the right "prescription" for your patient. When you have completed the proper questioning prior to the presentation then you can use **FFB** to present you product effectively.

FFB stands for Feature, Function and Benefit
A*n insurance agent may say something to the effect of... This is uninsured motorist protection coverage (Feature)*
It is going to protect you from drivers that are uninsured (Function)

The result is that with 15% of Americans still driving uninsured even if the driver is uninsured this coverage will cover not only the damage on your vehicle and the alternate party's vehicle, but it will also cover your deductible... Keeping you from having to come out of pocket due to another driver's negligence. (Benefit)

Which of course greatly minimizes your exposure...which based upon what you mentioned earlier is important to you, correct? (Tie Down question) Often times, sales professionals forget to speak about the benefit all together or they spend very little time discussing it or more time discussing features and functions... This should be the opposite. The majority of the time should be spent speaking about the benefits to the customer of your product or service...

2. The second **T** stands for **Tie-down**. A tie-down can be a rhetorical question, but it is essentially a statement with a question at the end. For instance, you may say, "And you like good gas mileage, don't you?" And, "Those wheels are nice, aren't they?" Those tie-down questions can get annoying, can't they? When doing that, even though it's a rhetorical question, you want to at least be able to get either a verbal answer from the customer, or at least allow their body language to dictate that they're in agreement. For instance, a head nod, or if you're over the phone you may notice a slight groan in agreement.

ALL IS FAIR IN LOVE AND SALES

Using tie-downs are extremely important because it is essentially like, when you are doing your presentation, say that a truck has a camper shell; when you take off that camper shell, then that leaves the bed of the truck exposed. When you're doing your presentation, you're putting a big piece of furniture in the bed of their truck. Put a big piece of furniture in there. These tie-down questions, such as, "And that's exactly what you were asking for, wasn't it?" "Then earlier you mentioned, that was something that was important to you, wasn't it?"

You want to draw back on things that they said earlier. "Earlier, you told me" is really the most powerful statement that you can make in either a presentation or a close. When you say, "Earlier, you mentioned fuel economy was important to you, and that's the reason why so many consumers are getting a Corolla. Do you think that you could use 40 miles to the gallon?" Those types of rhetorical questions and tie-downs are what will keep that "furniture" in place. Every question that you ask, you want to think of it like, there is now some spandex or a thin rope that is actually going from one side of the bed of the truck to the other. The more tie-downs that you use, the more secure the furniture is in there.

3. The next **T** stands for **Trial close**. Trial close. Trial closing is extremely, extremely imperative. At the end of your presentation, you want to be able to trial close. A trial close is essential dipping your toe in the water, testing it out, essentially getting the customer's temperature. One fairly archaic method that is often times used in automobile sales is, "Mister Customer, would you like to park that vehicle right over here in the sold line?" When you say, "Would you like to park it right over here in the sold line," then

it allows the customer an opportunity to say, "Wait a minute, I didn't say I was buying anything yet." Then it allows you an opportunity to ask the customer, "I'm sorry, why not?" So, you get an opportunity to sniff out that objection well before you actually get to the negotiation table. Because the last thing that you want to be doing in the heat of negotiation is having to handle objections. You want to isolate it to strictly the numbers.

Trial closing is extremely imperative because it can allow you to be able to sniff out an objection early on before you get to the numbers. Because if you wait to get to the numbers to handle an objection then virtually all that you can do often is discount your price in order to get the consumer to go ahead and move forward. When you isolate everything to where it's just the numbers, at this point in the presentation the consumer should not have seen yet, then that heightens your opportunity for closing, minimizes all of the other objections, because it allows you an opportunity to handle those objections prior to making it to the closing piece, and it ultimately makes for a swifter close, and a more concise close. Most importantly, it increases the probability that the deal will close.

Understanding and reading prospects' tonality, voice inflections, all those things can give you a strong inclination as to when to go for the close.

ALL IS FAIR IN LOVE AND SALES

ALL IS FAIR IN LOVE AND SALES

Chapter 3: Closing

The Art, The Science, and The Skill:

The first thing that's really imperative about closing is understanding your buyer. To understand your buyer, you want to understand the type of personality, and you want to understand what type of negotiator they are. When looking at potential buyers, there are five primary personality types according to Dustin Hillis, who is the co-founder of Southwestern Consulting and author of the book, *Navigate; Selling the Way that People Like to Buy.*

He refers to one personality type being an **Entertainer.** This is someone who often has a very gregarious personality, and their primary objective in the sales transaction is, they want to be liked. They want people to like them. One way to really appeal to this personality is to genuinely make them feel like they are the most interesting man or the most interesting woman on the planet. Because their primary objective is to be liked.

Another type is the **Detective**. The detective, they are very detail-oriented, the detectives are very fact-based, often they don't show a lot of emotion initially. They are more focused on, what are the facts, what are the figures, and what does that mean for me and my family? These people, you want to be very direct and factual in your approach, you don't want to leave out details that are important to them, and you really want to ensure that you don't speak in a lot of inferences and generalities, but you want to be as concise and factual as possible.

The next personality is the **Counselor**. The counselor. The counselor personality type is someone who really sees a lot of value in being able to have additional decision-makers. These people often will work in a group. These people will often bring additional decision-makers with them while they're potentially, during the transaction. They want to be sure that they bring additional buyers there, or additional people to help them make a decision. Teachers often times fit into this category. You really want to be able to understand that these are people that, you want to make them feel comfortable. They're usually the hippies of the world, and they are caring, loving, feeling and they're all about the emotion and if they feel your sincerity in their plight.

Next, you have the **Fighter**. The fighter is the person that is saying, "You aren't going to get over on me. You aren't going to get one over on me." These people are often times perceived as know-it-alls. With these people, their first inclination is to fight. These are not the sheep that you're going to be able to lead around and say, "Do this, do that." These are people that you're going to want to use inclusive terminology, such as, "How would you feel if we did this," or, "How would you feel if we did that?" You want to use words like "we" and "us". Because a fighter must feel like they're in control and they're the ones making the decisions. When a fighter feels like they're in control and they're making their decisions then they're often times much more inclined to go along with your suggestion because your suggestion has become their suggestion. With the fighter, it's really important to give the implication that they're in control, and you're essentially submitting to them. You want to maintain control without giving the implication that you're maintaining control.

Those are the four primary personality styles: Fighter, Entertainer, Counselor, and Detective. Throughout the sales process, you want to keep in mind, which personality type are you dealing with? That's going to help us to be able to craft closes and to know which one to use in our arsenal that's going to help us to be able to close it.

One other clue into the type of buyer that you may have is the consumer's occupation. To be fair, not all accountants, engineers, sales professionals, teachers...etc. think the same. However, understanding someone's occupation may give you some insight into their problem-solving process, or how they may justify or rationalize purchasing or not purchasing a product or service. This is the case because of "occupational conditioning". Which simply means that the longer we are involved in a particular occupation, the more it can "condition" the way we think. For instance, engineers, auditors, and accountants may be a little more analytical in their process, Police officers or business executives may be very blunt and direct and just want to get down to brass tax, whereas teachers or veterinarians may make their determination based upon just how they feel or based upon third party recommendations. When it comes to occupational conditioning, these things are by no means concrete. However, understanding the thought process that those professionals go through on a daily basis and how their secular environment may have conditioned them can give you insight into what closing statements, illustrations or analogies may particularly appeal to them.

Understanding the type of buyer that you have is one thing, however, you also want to be able to understand the type of negotiator that you have. To understand the type of negotiator that you have, there are five primary types of negotiators.

1: The first types are the people who do **Negotiation in Relation.** *Negotiation in Relation* means that this person negotiates in relation to their initial point of reference. For instance, if the professional says, "This costs $30," and the consumer automatically says without flinching, "I'll give you

20." These people are often times shooting from the hip, and they just negotiate in relation to whatever their initial point of reference was.

When dealing with someone who does negotiation in relation, it's imperative to be able to use what's called the law of contrasting principle. The law of contrasting principle can be summed up in 2 words... was-is. You may have seen this all around you throughout your life. You may have gone to your local department store and seen lawn mowers, and in big bold letters at the top, it says was $999 is $749. In order to negotiate with someone who negotiates in relation to whatever the initial price point is, it's imperative to change their initial point of reference.

For instance, an automotive sales professional may say that a vehicle price is set at $29,999, you may know, for some who've been in the automotive industry for quite some time, that the markup percentages at one point were up to 25%. Of course, they've shrunken in the new century; presently, the average markup is somewhere between 3% and 5% on a vehicle.

ALL IS FAIR IN LOVE AND SALES

For someone who negotiates in relation to the initial sticker price, you may tell that customer, "This vehicle would've been about $34,998, but what XYZ manufacturer has done, is they've reduced their profit margins even though the vehicle has more technology, just in order to stay competitively priced to the additional manufacturers. This vehicle would've been about $35,998 based upon the previous pricing model, but it's reduced down to $29,998.

What this does is changes a person's point of initial reference. The reason why this is so effective is something called the *Anchoring Effect*. The *Anchoring Effect*, in psychology, means that whatever the initial price that you associate with something, your brain automatically anchors the value of your product or service to whatever the initial price that you mentioned that it was. That's the value, that's your point of reference when it comes to value. Their value meter is anchored to whatever the initial price point that you mentioned.

2. The second type of negotiator is the **Win Negotiator**. The *Win Negotiator*, as the name implies, just want to win. They just want to win. In order to be effective with this type of negotiator, you have to give them the implication that they won. This is often someone who is competitive and strictly wants to feel like they got a deal. There, they don't stop until they feel like they have won, they have a deal. To win with this type of negotiator, you want to ensure that they feel that they have won... "You beat me down, you're a great negotiator, you win, I lose, and I'm going to acquiesce and go ahead and give you our bottom dollar." With the win negotiator, you want to be sure that they feel that they won.

3. The third type of negotiator is **Budget Negotiators**. *Budget Negotiators* whether you're dealing with a business to business prospect or a retail prospect, these are often honest people who just negotiate according to their budget. They just want to be able to fit your product or service into their budget. With these people, you often times can do a cost versus risk close. With these people, it's just a matter of helping them to understand how they can fit this into their budget, and how it's not an expenditure, rather an investment. Or how the additional money that they may

be spending either monthly or on a yearly basis is ultimately going to yield them additional revenue. You just want to help them work it out and help them fit it into their budget. Speak of the projected savings of your product or service over time or "reducing to the ridiculous" for these types of negotiators often works wonders! An example of reducing to the ridiculous is: $20 per month is really only $5 per week... or 1 less coffee from Starbucks per week (tying the leftover negotiation amount to something tangible such as a coffee often helps the budget negotiator to visualize something that they can live without and replace that expenditure with your product or service!) Even further $5 per week is really only .75 cent per day... or 1 less soda out of the vending machine each day! These are oftentimes a sales professional's favorite type of negotiators because they know that if they can justify the cost in the consumer's mind then they will have a sale!

4. The fourth type of negotiator is the **Research Negotiator**. This is the person who comes to your place of business to either purchase a home, or a car, or any transaction, they usually come with a little notebook or a little binder with lots of third-party information in there. What other people have paid for your product or service, reviews on your product or service, and questions regarding how this product or service compares to other products or services that are similar to yours, are some of the information contained.

This type of negotiator is oftentimes a salesperson's worst nightmare because they are often deemed as annoying, asking too many questions, digging in too deep, but it's important to win over this negotiator using transparency and 3rd party credibility. Transparency is so key for this type of negotiator. Oftentimes you want to use third-party credibility when closing this customer. If you're in automobile sales, you may use consumer reports, or a Kelley Blue Book to validate the reason why you're giving them X amount of dollars for your trade. This is extremely imperative.

Transparency is extremely important to this consumer and walking them through and validating their research. With the research negotiators, you want them to feel like they have done well, "I wish all of our customers came in educated and had done the amount of research that you've done because it makes our job a whole lot easier."

This is a bit of a paradigm shift from the last place this person was at, and they got the implication that they were annoying to the salesperson. When you validate their research and say, "As I'm sure that you've researched, Blank Mortgage is the best," or, "As I'm sure that you've researched, Kirby Vacuum Cleaner is the number one vacuum in the world," you want to validate their research, and use their research as leverage into your close. That's how you turn what would be most often dubbed as "annoying" to leverage their research into being able to close them.

5. Lastly are the **Value-based Negotiators**. The *Value-Based Negotiators* are the optimal customers for most industries. Because the *Value-Based Negotiator* negotiates based upon their perception of value. Sometimes the value-based negotiators have more money, but they just negotiate in relation to their perception of value. If you do a great presentation, a great introduction, a great presentation, and you bring out the facts and figures, you can pick on their hot buttons and what it is that's important to them, then they will pay you top dollar based upon their perception of value. With these people, it's important to do a good introduction and ask probing questions to give a solid presentation. These types of negotiators will pay the money if they see the value!

Those are some points regarding understanding their personality types, so you can use analogies and closes that appeal to them, and secondly understanding the type of negotiator that you're entering a potential negotiation with will help you to be able to close faster and more efficiently by having crafted closes for each negotiation style.

The entitlement theory just means that people are more inclined to take an offer that they feel like they're entitled to, as opposed to something that you are offering them, that is optional.

For instance, there's an automobile salesperson who goes to the service department, and asks a customer, "Would you like to test drive a new vehicle?" The customer may or may not say yes. But if you take that same customer and you go back there and you ask them, "Hey mister customer, I apologize, have you already received your complimentary vehicle presentation today?"

Because I phrased it in a manner that sounds like this is something that they were already entitled to, but had not yet received, it increases the chances that the consumer is going to go ahead and take you up on that for. Because nobody wants to be entitled to something and not receive it.

A perfect example of this is, I was in Vancouver, Canada, and I was at a restaurant where there was a company who had what looked to be young college kids in there, and the college kids were going around with something called an app for an app. If you downloaded this application on your phone, then you could get a free appetizer at the restaurant. It was their way of getting people exposed to their mobile application.

I went in there and I was picking up my food, and what I observed was that the kids were going up and saying,

"Would you mind downloading your application? You could get a free appetizer." They were getting shut down left and right. Everybody was like, "No, I'm okay, no, I'm okay, no, and I'm okay." appetizer at the restaurant. It was their way of getting people exposed to their mobile application.

As I watched this go on, what I realized is that they could say the same information maybe in a slightly different manner, and you will get a completely different result. I huddled all the kids around me and I said, "Hey guys, here's what you should say. 'Mister Customer, have you already received your complimentary appetizer?'

The customer is, of course, going to say no. Then you want to ask them, 'If you were to get an appetizer, what would you get? Would you get the chocolate cake, would you get the molten lava cake, or would you get the cheesecake?' Let them choose their appetizer. Afterwards say, 'Great, I'll go ahead and get that started for you. By the way, all that you need to do to get your free appetizer is just download this application. Download this application and I'll go ahead and get that appetizer started for you.'"

ALL IS FAIR IN LOVE AND SALES

In doing this, the next wave of customers that came in that they tried this technique on, all downloaded this application on their phone. The reason why that worked, is because the kids got them to first feel like they were entitled to something that they didn't receive. Secondly, they got the customers to visualize themselves eating an appetizer from the menu by having them to pick something out. Lastly, the kids told the customers what they needed to do to obtain the appetizer in which they had already visualized.

What a powerful sales technique to utilize the "entitlement theory" to obtain the desired result. This technique also works very well with door-to-door sales. I was providing some sales training and coaching for a roofing company and I encouraged the roofing sales professional to consider this approach "Mister Customer, I apologize that it took me so long to get out here. We were just up working with your neighbors here and found a little bit of roof damage that we are fixing for them. (Obviously the roofing sales person was to only say this statement if it was true that the sales person or his organization was working on a roof in the neighborhood).

He could further go on to say, "There were some storms in the area earlier. There was some damage on some of your neighbors' roof, and what we're doing is, complimentary roof inspections for the entire neighborhood as a courtesy. I just wanted to be sure that you had received yours." In doing that, he didn't ask for the close, he didn't ask, "Can I give you a complimentary roof inspection," he asked, "Have you already received your roof inspection that you're essentially "entitled" to?"

What he found is that this increased the percentage of homes that he completed roof assessments for by nearly 30%, and he increased his closing ratio by 28%. Which led to him making about $4,000 extra per month, just by making that one slight alteration. Similar strategies work for door to door sales and many other industries that require an assessment prior to a sales presentation: Mortgage- a complimentary home value assessment to see if there is perhaps enough equity to facilitate a refinance.

Automotive: a complimentary vehicle appraisal to determine if now is the optimal time to trade. Or a complimentary product demonstration (test drive) especially when speaking with customers who are waiting for their vehicle to be serviced in the service lounge.

Insurance agents may give a complimentary coverage analysis to ensure that the prospect has the right coverage for their needs but also see if there is an opportunity to get the consumer to switch providers...

I believe that you get the picture...

Another thing that's important to understand when it comes to closing is what's called **Occupational Conditioning**. *Occupational Conditioning* means that people's occupations can sometimes condition them to think a certain way. When closing, it's important to be able to use all of the tools that you have available, one of which is a person's occupation. For instance, engineers are often more analytical, so that allows you to be able to use closes and analogies that are more suited to their way of thinking.

Teachers often have a bit of a counselor personality, and they may prefer additional decision makers. For teachers, it may be important for them to feel like they are not alone in their decision-making process by using the **Principle of Consensus**. The *principle of consensus*, according to Dr Robert Cialdini, is one of the six primary principles of human influence. The **Principle of Consensus** simply states that people want to do the things that other people are doing. To close someone with that type of "counselor personality", it may behoove you to make that decision maker a part of a larger control group, for instance, you may say "Last year alone, we sold over X amount of this product or service to customers just like yourself." For this personality type, it can make the step of moving forward less intimidating because there are now examples of so many people that have moved forward also.

Understanding someone's occupation can give you insights into the best ways to close them!

Great closers have an **ear** for closing. Yes, they're good listeners, but by **ear** I mean **E-A-R.**
The **E** stands for **Education**. *Education* just means that great closers take the time to educate themselves on not only their product, but also people. They're all for continuous education and perfecting their craft. They often have coaches, and people to help continuously educate them about

themselves and to give them a vested outside perspective into themselves and their business. One of my favorite quotes from Jim Rohn said that "A formal education will make you a living, but a self-education will make you a fortune." Being able to educate yourself on your product, your service, and educating yourself on the art and the skill of closing is really what separates the good from the great.

The **A** stands for **Analytics**. Great closers have analytics surrounding their closing. They don't just say, "I'm a great closer, I close quite a few deals." The best of the best know what their closing ratios are because they track them. There is an adage that says that you can't manage what you don't measure. Great closers know what their closing ratios are under certain situations. They know what their closing ratio is on different subsets or distinct groups and also on products or services within different price points. Great closers may say things such as on "Everything $50,000 and over my closing ratio is this, everything $30,000 over my closing ratio is this."

Being able to monitor your closing ratio is extremely important. Know the analytics surrounding it. For instance, an automobile salesperson may monitor what their closing ratio is when an appraisal is done upfront as opposed to when they do the appraisal at a different date, or later in the sales process. To be a great closer it is imperative to know the analytics surrounding your closing ratio's, and to monitor your ratios. There's an adage that says that you can't manage what you don't measure, and what you don't track. Track your closing ratios as well as your situational closing ratios.

The **R** in having an **EAR** for closing stands for **Repetition**. Great closers have lots of repetition. They thrust themselves into as many closing situations as possible, because they know that the more they put into the fire, the better they're going to get. Many people liken repetition to having a callous on your hand. When you first get that callous it may hurt a little bit, it may sting, it may be uncomfortable, but as that skin becomes calloused, then it essentially loses sensitivity. Same way in sales. The more repetitions that you have, the less sensitive you become if something regarding that deal goes awry, if you lose the deal, or if a customer gives you an unexpected objection. You become less sensitive and more focused, and essentially a better closer. The more repetitions that you have, the more of an expert you become.

In closing, it's important to have what many refer to as a poker face. A poker face doesn't mean that you don't smile, that you aren't happy. It just means that you don't show emotions such as disdain, discomfort, anger, or frustration when something doesn't go your way in a close. It's important to have a poker face and to not show anger or frustration to your consumer.

It is also essential to read buying signals from the customer, as well as your body language and the prospects body language. Some buying signals to be mindful of may consist of realizing and acknowledging when a customer is asking you questions that mention them already using your product or service.

In automobile sales, they may say, "Would I just bring it here to get serviced, or would I bring it to another dealership?" That's a buying signal. A consumer who is, purchasing a home may tell the real estate agent, "When my son goes to school in the neighborhood would the buses pick him up in the front of the house or only at the neighborhood bus stop?" That's a buying signal.

A Mortgage broker, or loan officer may be trying to close a customer on doing a refinance on their home, then that consumer may ask the question, "Would I still have the same payment due date, or would I be able to change that?" What an inexperienced salesperson may do is talk past the close, answer that question, and feel like they must keep selling. But what a closing savant would do is understand that now is the time to go for the close, and they are going to go for the close after reading the buying signals.

Another key factor is body language, both the prospects as well as your own. You want to pay attention to your prospects body language and pay attention to yours. When reading body language, it's important to understand a few things.

The first thing is, humans, have what's called a baseline. A baseline in body language just means a persons

ALL IS FAIR IN LOVE AND SALES

natural tendencies, like twitches or certain things that they do out of nervousness. Many may mistake this as having some type of hidden meaning however that may not be the case. It's important to establish a customer's baseline, or what they usually do in their natural motions first, and then notice alterations in those behavioral patterns as you say certain things, or as you move along in the sales process. Understanding body language is crucial in the selling process.

When a customer folds their arms, it could really be cold in there, or it could mean that they're feeling closed off and they're not open or interested in hearing what you have to say right now. Often, to get the prospect to be more openminded again, a sales professional may ask their customer something about their kids, or something about something that's familiar to them, or near and dear to them, to get them to open back up.

Also, you want to pay attention to the direction that your customer's feet is pointing. The direction that a prospects feet are pointing will usually give a good indication of where their body wants to go. Often, you'll notice, when people get ready to leave a place and they're sitting down, their feet will begin to point in that direction, because they want to go. Meaning they're entire body or at least their feet will point to the left or to the right or whichever way of the door. If you notice that their feet are pointing away from you or began to point toward the door it's important to utilize that information and it just may be time to get into the close quickly, and efficiently. At the least at that point it may be best to re-engage your customer and get them to want to stay.

Lastly, you want to pay attention to the eyes. Take notice of the arms, feet, and eyes. The eyes, sometimes, can mislead us. They probably move the most out of all our body members. A couple of rules of thumb regarding the eyes: when people are looking up and to the left, it often is for recollection, but if someone is continuously looking to the left when they're saying statements, maybe it's about their financial situation, or maybe it's about something slightly uncomfortable, then it could potently mean maybe they're embellishing something. Perhaps they're not being truthful.

ALL IS FAIR IN LOVE AND SALES

If the eyes are shifty, continuously look down or if they can't make eye contact, they're constantly looking to the left that may mean that there's a sign of either discomfort or distrust when it comes to them making eye contact with you.

Also, in closing, something that's imperative to remember is silence. Silence is your friend. Don't be afraid to use silence to your advantage. Often, people feel like they must fill the silence with something. Some type of statement, just something, they must fill that silence with something. What they don't realize is that, when closing, silence could be your greatest closer. Silence could be your greatest closer because silence allows you to let the customer speak first. They can give you their objection or their agreement. And it keeps you from talking way past the sale. You may use one of the closes that we're about to get into, and then shut up, and let the customer speak first. In a negotiation, there's an adage that says he who speaks first loses.

I could write an entire book based on closing alone, but for people especially interested in closing more business, I encourage you to email the email address on the back of the book, and book a consultation with me regarding our sales coaching. For now, I want to go over three of my favorite types of closes. But before I do, I want to emphasize the importance of being concise in the close.

A close should not end with a plethora of options. This can induce what's commonly referred to, in sales psychology, as paralysis by analysis. Simply put, it just means that when faced with too many options, often decision makers become "paralyzed" in a sense meaning that they hold off and don't make any decision... rather they just revert to that which is comfortable to them... which is no, or they may say... "You gave me lots to think about... do you have a business card?" If you have done a proper introduction and asked appropriate probing questions, then you shouldn't have to give a litany of options at the end but should be able to suggest or narrow things down to a few options based upon your expertise and the information that the prospect has provided.

A few of the most effective closes that I have found are:

ALL IS FAIR IN LOVE AND SALES

1. The second is the **No-Means-Yes Close**. The no-means-yes close. I've heard it called a lot of different things, but Rory Vaden, who is a world thought leader in time management and sales and in leadership, calls it the no-means-yes close. The no-means-yes close, simply put, just means that sometimes we are conditioned to say no to things, and so this close causes the brain to think a little bit differently. We're going to use the no-means-yes close, which is asking a question inversely. Instead of asking a customer, "Would you do business with me?" I'm going to ask the consumer, "Can you think of any reason why we couldn't go ahead and move forward?"

When they say, "No, I can't think of any reason why we shouldn't move forward," they are in turn saying yes. We're turning that no into a yes. This is a bit of a psychological mechanism, and it causes people to really think about reasons why they shouldn't move forward. If they can't think of any reason why they shouldn't move forward, then it makes "yes" the obvious option. We're turning that no into yes.

2. The next is a **Choice of Two Positives** The choice of two positives, simply put, is usually either-or. No matter which one of these choices that the customer chooses, either one is going to be beneficial to you. If I'm a stockbroker, I may ask the consumer, "Did you want to go ahead and do 45 shares of the red stock or 45 shares of the blue stock?" An automotive sales professional may ask the customer, "Did you want your payments 30 days out or 45 days?" If I'm a real estate agent, I may ask the potential home buyer prospect, "Did you want to go ahead and go with the house on 5th Street or the house on 6th Street as far as the one that you're making your offer on?" The choice of two positives is simply taking the yes or no out of the equation, and just allowing them to choose between the choice of two positives.

3. Lastly is the **Visualization Close**. The visualization close is where you get the customer to visualize themselves using your product or service. The visualization close If you're again doing automobile sales, you may ask the prospect, "Who's the first person that you're going to show this thing off to? Are you going to drive this vehicle

ALL IS FAIR IN LOVE AND SALES

down highway 45 then get on highway 30 to go home? How fast are you going to drive?"

I'm getting the customer to visualize themselves using my product or service. Similarly, this works with real estate sales. One may ask the consumer, "How many people are you going to have over in this home? When are you going to have your first house party? Do you think you're going to do it on the first month or the second month? What type of decorations are you going to use?" This is in turn getting the customer to visualize using your product or service and so goes the visualization close.

The art of closing is really like painting a beautiful Picasso when you see all your work finally come together. The art is being able to understand signals even when a customer tries to hold them in. Looking at their words, their body language, knowing when the right time to go for the close is, and then it's like shooting the bull's eye with the bow and arrow. You must stabilize the bow, monitor the wind speed, and let the arrow go just at the right time to hit the bull's eye. Closing is the exact same way.

The art of closing consist of anticipating potential objections prior to them even coming up, effective questioning prior to the presentation, and tailoring your presentation to the prospects needs. Closing then becomes a mere formality. People who have mastered the art of closing often are referred to as naturals or people who just close naturally. This naturalness however, is often a learned behavior, whether consciously or subconsciously. The art of closing combines the science and psychology of sales and decision making, with the presentation skills without having to lie, cheat, or steal and the result is a beautiful masterpiece.

ALL IS FAIR IN LOVE AND SALES

ALL IS FAIR IN LOVE AND SALES

ALL IS FAIR IN LOVE AND SALES

Chapter 4: Objection Handling

"Turning No into Now."

Real objection versus Stated Objection, versus Condition. To properly overcome objections, you must first, be able to determine if you have one. To do this, it's important to understand the difference between a stated objection, a real objection and a condition created by an objection. A condition, is simply, a condition created by an objection. An example of a condition is, "No, thanks or I'm just not ready to buy right now."

A **condition** doesn't have a reason directly attached to it; it's often simply a "yes" or "no". You cannot overcome a condition, so it is important to get past the "no", or "I'm just not ready to buy" by quite simply asking...Why?

A **stated objection** is oftentimes referred to as a "smokescreen". This is an objection, that, a prospect may throw out just to get out of the selling situation. This type of objection, usually, is to relieve the prospect from the selling situation but is not the actual objection or the real reason that the customer won't move forward. Oftentimes, there is a real objection behind it. For instance, a prospect directly after seeing the cost may say, "Oh sorry, I ran out of time." The real objection? "After seeing the numbers, I feel like the price is too high." A prospect may say, "I need to speak to my spouse."

The real objection; "I don't see enough value in your product to go ahead and make a decision." To decipher if it is a stated objection it is important to ask additional questions and to use the RIO technique that is outlined in the next chapter.

A real objection, is just that. A real objection as to why a prospect does not want to move forward. These are often very direct, such as, "The Price is too high" or "There's a different product or service that appeals to me more."

How to decide the difference between the objections you're getting, is to ask additional questions. You know you are dealing with a condition that is created by an objection if you can't put the words, "the reason why I don't want to purchase now is because," at the beginning of that condition and have the statement have an adequate "cause and effect." An example of this is, "The reason why I don't want to purchase is because of No Thanks". That's not an adequate "cause and effect", so you know it's a condition. Another example of that is "I don't want to purchase right now because I am not ready to buy right now" That is again not adequate cause and effect and doesn't' give a reason as to why the customer is not ready to move forward. Therefore, it's important to ask questions until you get a proper cause and effect, such as "I don't have the money right now, or I am still considering other products…etc

Stated objections are often discovered by *reducing to the ridiculous.* For example, someone may give you the objection: "Oh, I'm sorry, I'm out of time, so that's why I can't move forward right now." So, one way to overcome that objection is to reduce to the ridiculous by saying "Ma'am, if I were to make you a deal that you absolutely couldn't refuse, would that be worth taking a few extra moments to wrap this up?" Or, "If I could at least have the primary signature portion of the purchase wrapped up in five minutes, would that suffice for you?" If time is the real objection then the deal should probably close then and there. If time isn't the real objection, then they may say something like... "Well, it's also the numbers as well. I just need to think about them." (AKA... The price is too high). Additional questions are paramount when discovering if you are dealing with a real objection or a stated objection. The objective is to turn every no, whether it is a condition or a stated objection into a real objection that you can overcome. Once that transition takes place then you can use the following formula.

The formula for objection handling is **R-I-O**. That stands **for "Restate, Isolate" and "Overcome"**.

- **Restate**. To be sure you have the correct understanding, "Restate" the objection or the thought that you felt the prospect was trying to convey. This shows empathy if done with the right tonality, and, helps to ensure that you have the proper understanding prior to handling the objection. You can start the sentence off by saying, "Mr. Customer, just to be sure I understand you correctly, the reason why you don't feel comfortable moving forward is ____." So, you want to restate it in a soft and empathic tone as if you were genuinely trying to acquire additional understanding to be sure that their needs are met.

- **"Isolate."** After you restating the objection you then want to isolate it. To do this you may say something such as; "Mr. Prospect, aside from (insert the objection that you just received) would there be anything else to keep you from moving forward today?" Ensure that only this one objection remains. Once this is accomplished, then you know that you're one objection away from home. One objection away from closing the sale.
- **"Overcome."** This is a step that most novice professionals like to skip to. This is the portion where you give the prospect reasons why the they should still move forward despite their objection. But you shouldn't

give all the reasons at once as closing is not about giving all the facts and figures as to why a prospect should move forward. Rather, it is about showing empathy, understanding, and consideration towards your prospect, and helping to guide them to a decision. Think of overcoming the objection like a sniper as opposed to someone using a machine gun. Use personalized and tailored facts as opposed to just spouting all the reasons why the prospect should move forward. This allows you to keep a few "bullets" in your gun if need be to close the sale and it also helps to keep the customer from feeling pressured by you spouting fact after fact in rapid succession.

"Feel", "Felt", "Found".

One effective way to illustrate empathy and consideration for your prospect to use the Feel, Felt, Found when transitioning into your close...You may tell a customer, "Mr. Customer, I understand how you **FEEL**. I once **FELT**

ALL IS FAIR IN LOVE AND SALES

the same way. But here is what I **FOUND** with a little bit further research." Or "I understand how you feel. A previous client once felt the same way, but here's what they found with a little bit further research." Transitioning into your close this way is one way to show empathy and help the prospect see that you aren't just trying to force or pressure them into purchasing your product or service but that you actually care.

One of the most effective closes to use when overcoming an objection is called the relevant story close.

Relevant Story Close. A relevant story close just means using a relevant story of another prospect who may have had the same or a similar objection that purchased your product or service and how well it worked out for them. The relevant story close can be broken down into 3 stages P.S.P:

- **P- Personalize.** The way to personalize a story is to draw parallels between the character in your story and that character's situation and the decision maker in front of you and their current situation.

- **S- Situation.** This is the part where you tell the story or the "situation" and the happenings of that story as it relates to your current prospect.

- **P- Pain or Reward.** This is the end of the story where you discuss the pain or reward of the previous prospect moving forward with your product or service. The pain that the customer experienced by not moving forward or the reward that the customer experienced by moving forward.

For example: Perhaps a financial advisor is advising a prospect to invest with his firm and the client says the objection, "I will just hold off because I don't have lots of available cash right now. So, I will just maybe wait until next year." After re-stating, then isolating the objection, the financial advisor may then use a relevant story close as follows:

Personalize- "You know, Mr. Prospect, I can understand how you feel that way. You remind me a lot of Charles

ALL IS FAIR IN LOVE AND SALES

Smith. Much like you, he had children, had recently moved over to a new job and didn't have much to invest. So, he thought about just waiting until he had more money also."

Situation- "However, when I shared with him the benefits of even investing just 20 dollars per week. He thought about it and said… 'that's less than 5 dollars per day. I can pack my lunch instead of eating out every day for lunch and save that.' So, he decided to invest with us $20 per week."

Pain or Relief- "What he found was that after just 1 year of investing with us, not only did he receive a 300% return on his money but also he is getting a raise at his job due to being there for 1 year. He plans on keeping his lifestyle the same in just using his raise to go directly into his investment portfolios. He stated that had he not started off with $20 per week and seen the possibilities with that small amount then he wouldn't be able to invest his entire salary difference into investments. He still thanks me to this day for encouraging him to start small and helping him to see the possibilities. His investment portfolio has grown so much and he even says that now he sleeps better now that he knows that he is securing his family's financial future…He says that $20 per week changed the trajectory of his life and his family's financial future. "Can you see why many people invest with us even if it starts as low as $20 per week?"

Once the prospect answers yes to that question you can then transition directly into a close such as... "Great... Did you want your first investments to come out on the next Monday or would Tuesday be better?" Or "Great, can you think of any reason why you wouldn't want to receive those same benefits as Charles did and go ahead and get started today?"

This is just one of many closes that I have trained and coached sales and leadership professionals all over North America on. The psychology of why this close is particularly effective is because when you start off the story by drawing similarities from the prospect to the character in the story what happens is that as the story progresses, subconsciously the prospect replaces the character in the story with themselves, so they feel pain or the reward of the ending of the story. Therefore when they get out of this story in their imagination and have to come back to reality, they no longer have the security of having your product or service as it was illustrated in the story so this motivates them to move forward. This is called subconscious implementation.

Cost vs Investment Close

Another close that can be used is the **Cost vs Investment Close**: This close works well for any product or service that is being sold to help with efficiencies or that can be viewed as an investment... This may be a realtor convincing an apartment lessee that purchasing a home instead would be better, or a software sales professional illustrating how spending money to automate certain tasks is really not a cost but an investment or a multi-level marketing professional illustrating how investing in the start-up cost of their business can make the prospect lots of money in the future.

This close can perhaps be used when a prospect states that they don't have the money, but you know that the money is there it is just a matter of re-allocating funds for your product or service and you know that this is the best thing for the prospect!

An example of this close is, "Mrs. Prospect, if I asked you for twenty dollars each day, but at the end of the month, I said, 'I'm going to give you thirty dollars for every twenty dollars that you gave me at the end of the month,' would you find a way to give me that twenty dollars?"

Mrs. Customer - "Yes."

"Perfect, well, Mrs. Customer, that's exactly what we're speaking about today. By investing in our product this isn't a cost... rather an investment into (yourself or your business or your future... whichever is applicable) just like you would find a way to give me that $20 per day to get $30 back; that is essentially what you're doing by investing in our product here today. Because of this product or service increasing your _____ or saving you time by _____ then it will essentially be like giving $20 per day and getting back $30 at the end. Can you see the parallels?

Customer - "Yes."

You: "Great. So, do you want to go ahead and take 'Package A?' Or 'Package B?'".

The Pivot Close:

The pivot close involves using the exact reason why the customer doesn't want to move forward as the reason why they should. For instance, when selling sales coaching and training services, a prospect may say, "Well, I just don't have the money right now." One, can then, "pivot" that objection, by using that as the exact reason why they should move forward, by saying, "Well, Mr. Customer, I can understand that you feel that you don't have the money right now." In fact, that's the exact reason why many customers have moved forward with us, because, they want to be able to increase their sales skills to be able to make more money. They asked themselves that if they didn't have the money now...then what would change in the future if they didn't change their sales skills and the habits surrounding their business and that's the reason why some even borrowed money to have access to our world class sales training and coaching services because they knew that it was a luxury for their business... It is a necessity! Can you see how the fact that you don't have the money right now is exactly why you need this?"

Similarly, this close works for lots of different industries. Sometimes it's important to realize and to consider that the prospects objection may be the very problem that your product solves. Sometimes you simply have to convey that to the prospect!

ALL IS FAIR IN LOVE AND SALES

ALL IS FAIR IN LOVE AND SALES

Chapter 5: Referrals

Referrals, Referrals, Referrals:

First, we're going to talk about why referrals are important. Referrals are important because as the title implies, it allows you to get more business, and more prospects, with less effort than having to continuously cold call a prospect for more business. There's also what's called a "Trust transfer". The relationship or trust, at least in part, is handed over from the referrer to the referred.

Trust is essential in sales and statistics show that referrals are directly related to shortening the sales cycle and increasing sales. Some statistics show that a fifty to sixty percent increase in closing ratio can be directly contributed to referrals over non-preferred prospects.

If someone asked you the question, "How would you like to increase your business by fifty percent?" What would the obvious answer be? "Absolutely!" Referrals are important, not only because of increased closing percentages, but also because of business sustainability.

One way to increase your business, minimize income fluctuation, and continuously grow, is through referrals. I can remember being in automobile sales, with a sales representative by the name of, Adam Minkley, who was great at this. Each year, I would watch him have to stand outside in the heat and cold, less and less as he built up his referral network.

Another reason referrals are important is time management. If you're able to spend more of your time with qualified prospects that have a higher propensity to do business with you due to the trust transference of a referral, the amount of money you make each hour, just went up. Your time just became more valuable. You can spend less time working, and more time enjoying family, etc. Time is the most valuable commodity on the planet. We're always spending it and can never get it back. Use. Yours. Wisely. Who should you get referrals from? Well, the answer to that is short; Everyone. Friends and family, clients, past clients...everyone!

At Southwestern Consulting, one of the first things that we would encourage a new client to do is to make a "Hot One-Hundred" list. This list wasn't only potential prospects that were in their existing network, but one-hundred or more people who were friends, family and/or associates that would answer the client's phone call. How could this help? Well, your friends and family, and phone contacts, are some of the people who are most willing to point you in the right direction to give you the name, and phone number, of some potential prospects that are in their existing network (aka referrals!)

Oftentimes, we may scroll through our phone and look for the people, only in related businesses to get referrals from and miss out on people within our own network, who could be holding the key, to additional clients for your business. So, the first place to look for referrals is from those closest to you and those who want to help you the most. You may find that you inadvertently even turn your friends and/or family into clients just because you asked them for referrals and made them conscious of your product or service.

Other referral sources may come from related businesses, businesses that sell to the same industry; their decision makers, current clients, past clients and one of the most commonly missed ones, even from the customers who tell you "No." When a product or service is not a great fit for an individual or business, don't miss the opportunity to ask them for referrals. You can turn one "No" into lots of "Yeses"

How to get more Referrals?

Ask, ask, and ask. The primary reason why most professionals, and entrepreneurs, don't get more referrals is simply that they don't ask. One survey says that less than twenty percent of sales professionals, ask for referrals. Now, there's also a statistic that shows that twenty percent of the salespeople make eighty percent of the money, I can almost guarantee, that, these top twenty percent earners are asking for, and gathering, referrals. Oftentimes at the risk of not

ALL IS FAIR IN LOVE AND SALES

seeming "cool", or feeling burdensome, many sales professionals, don't ask. This may call for a shift in mindset.

You must ask yourself, "Is my product or service really valuable?" "Are there people's lives who would be better with my product or service?" "Do people need this?" If you answered "Yes" to any of these questions, then ask for referrals often and shamelessly.

How to ask for Referrals?

Ask broadly and ask specifically. One way to do this is to ask for people in a particular situation, as well as, just people in general. This technique is called the Broad-Specific Referral Technique.

As the name implies this technique asks for the referral starting broad and then gets more specific. For instance, a roofing salesperson may ask, "Mr. Customer, do you know anyone who lives in a storm-ridden area?" (allow for response) The roofing salesperson may continue... "Or maybe even anyone else who owns a home with a roof on it? (That last question may elicit a chuckle because if said with the right tonality can be perceived as a joke because of course virtually every house has a roof on it...lol). Which should also make the referrals a no-brainer as well.

What this technique prompts you to do is to ask both specifically for someone that is in a particular situation, which in this example is perhaps someone in a storm-ridden area, and then broadly. Which in this example is, anyone that owns a home with a roof on it. This should allow you to receive referrals to people in a current situation where your product could be beneficial and people who may need your services at some point in the future and everyone in between...This technique can put prospects in your immediate pipeline as well as prospects in your future pipeline that may become your clients later later.

Reverse Prospecting Referral Technique

When it comes to asking for referrals from related businesses or organizations, few techniques are more effective than *"Reverse Prospecting"*. *Reverse Prospecting* is a technique that really puts the potential referral partner's interests ahead of your own. Reverse Prospecting means that

ALL IS FAIR IN LOVE AND SALES

you're going to call on a business, or an organization that, may have some type of relation to your business, or you guys may be able to send each other reciprocal referrals.

For instance a reverse prospecting script for a real estate professional may go something like this if they are calling wedding planner for instance:

You- "Hello, Jon, it's Chris. Chris over here at X-Y-Z Mortgage. The reason why I was calling you is because I was looking through my referral book, and, I realized that one of the number one reasons why people buy a new home is because of a major change in their lifestyle, such as marriage, and I realized that I don't actually have a good wedding planner to refer my clients to. Would you be okay if I were to send you some business?"

*Referral Partner-*Yes! Absolutely

You- "Cool! Can you tell me a little bit about what separates you guys apart over there at X-Y-Z Wedding Planners?" (Listen to the response... This allows the referral partner prospect to "sell" you on their services and may give you some insight into what to say to a client of yours that you may be sending over for a referral when the time comes. This also makes the referral partner prospect more likely to listen to you when you are telling them about your product or service).

Referral partner prospect- "Well, we are, Number One in customer satisfaction, and we can help them plan a wedding anywhere!"

You- "Great, that sounds exactly like the type of person I am looking to partner with. Are you still over there on Beach Street?"

Referral partner prospect- "Yes."

You- "Perfect. I'm going to be over in that area on Monday at Two O'clock, and Wednesday, at Five O'clock. Which one of those times works best for me to stop by? Perhaps we can grab lunch or a coffee in that area and I can get some cards from you, learn a little more about your business and also drop off some of my cards and let you know a little bit about what we do over here at X-Y-Z Mortgage? Which one of those times works best for you, Monday or Wednesday?"

Referral partner prospect- "Monday at 2 O'clock and there is a Starbucks here on Beach Street!"

You- "Okay, perfect, I'll be there Monday at 2 O'clock. What's your email address? I'll shoot you a quick calendar invitation to be sure the time is protected in both of our calendars."

Now, Eighty to Ninety percent of that call, was focused on the prospect, and me giving them new business, and only ten to twenty percent of the call was focused on myself, and me getting business. So, when you think of asking for referrals, you want to be conscious of how you can send referrals and **give to get**. Reverse prospecting can change everything you know, about getting referrals and make getting referrals easier than ever before!

Networking Referrals:

At networking events, it's extremely imperative, to be sure that you show interest first, and ask for business second. Ask questions such as "How can I help your business? What types of customers would benefit you the most if I sent them your way?" Learning about someone else's business is the best way to show interest in them, and, interest in their products or service, to elicit interest in your own services. You want to be interested in their business and pull out your mobile device and check your calendar and book a meeting or a networking lunch or coffee right then and there if you can because if the card simply goes in the pocket then often the meeting never happens!

Social Media Referral technique:

Leveraging social media is extremely important when it comes to getting referrals.

At referral coffees or lunches, Novice sales professionals will ask: "Who do you know?" Elite sales and business professionals will ask: "How do you know?" The only way that you can ask "how do you know" is by coming into the referral meeting prepared. This is imperative because we can ask someone who they know that they may be able to refer us to and often, the answer could be, "Oh, let me think about it." Or "I don't know right now."

When you ask the referral partner a question such as, "These are a few people that I was going to reach out to and I noticed that you were connected with them on LinkedIn… How do you know (First Name on the List)?" Let the referral partner tell you, as this allows you to be able to ask the follow-up question, "What is something you like or respect the most about them?" (Allow for a response). If they are struggling to answer that question, then you may be able to ask the referral partner what is one interesting fact about this person that they are connected to? This allows you to get what we call at Southwestern Consulting a Golden Nugget. And lastly, the question that you ask to be sure that you have permission is… "Mr. Referral Partner, when I do speak with _____ Do you mind if I share with him some of the good things that you said about him?" The referral partner most oftentimes will of course say, "Sure, you can!" This gives you permission to use that referrals partner's name when calling this referral. You will also be able to leverage some interesting piece of information, or some compliment that you obtained from your referral partner about your new prospect and increase your chances of turning that new prospect into a new client!

One of my favorite examples of this is, I was marketing my training services, to a dealership, and upon receiving a referral, I asked my referral partner, "Hey, what's something you like or respect the most about the person that you are referring me to?" And he said, "Well, that is a tough question. A few moments of silence passed so, I then transitioned to, "Well, what's an interesting fact that you know about him?" He then said, "An interesting fact is that he likes Batman much better than Superman." So, no doubt, in calling him, my first statement was, "Hey look, you don't know me, I don't know you, but pffft, Superman is way better than Batman." That no doubt, sparked a lively discussion filled with laughter and the appointment was set. That's the importance of not only asking for the referral, but also getting the "Golden Nugget" or additional pre-approach and taking that referral 1 step further!

ALL IS FAIR IN LOVE AND SALES

For Multilevel marketing organizations or business to consumer sales... This same technique can be applied using Facebook or other forms of social media!

ALL IS FAIR IN LOVE AND SALES

Chapter 6: Follow up

Post-sale follow-up

Follow up and follow-through to success. Proper follow up is important to develop and is often times forgotten. Love them and leave them, unfortunately, is what many sales professionals live by. In fact, some statistics show that after a purchase, even the purchase of a big-ticket item like a car or a home, the consumer often doesn't even remember the sales professional's name within 1 year's time.

One of the facts that make this reality such a travesty is because statistics also show that consumers in general are 44% more likely to say yes again after they have done business with a person before. So, existing clients or past clients are not only are not only great referral partners, but they can become champions of you, your business, and what you sell in the community and repeat customers for years to come. If you follow up often and purposely. They can help draw consumers to your business. Follow-up is the final, and one of the most important keys to success. For some people, it's a birthday card each year. For others, it's gifts to celebrate the anniversary of the date of purchase.

One of my favorite examples of this was Joe Girard, who is widely regarded as the top automotive salesperson in the history of automotive sales. He is currently in the Guinness Book of World Records for selling 1,425 automobiles in 1973. To this day that is still the automotive sales record for 1 calendar year of individual automotive sales. What he did was, on every birthday, every anniversary, even the children's birthday, he would send out a handwritten thank you card or handwritten birthday card each year. He would often have customers lined up in the lobby. They would only deal with him for their purchase. He created, what many people consider to be a bit of a cult following primarily because he was so good at follow-up. And once a customer was in his web or they purchased one car from him, the likelihood was that they would purchase many, many more.

ALL IS FAIR IN LOVE AND SALES

So, whether it is an anniversary of the purchase date, a wedding anniversary, or quarterly check-ups ... whatever your method is, simply have one. Follow up often and with a purpose. One way to look at each consumer is like they are a long-term, lifelong relationship.

Whether you're selling insurance, mortgage loans, real estate, financial planning, automobiles, etc. ... calculate your customers' monetary value by simply multiplying the amount of projected business that that consumer will purchase over time multiplied by the number of projected referrals that you could obtain on average each time someone buys your product.... For instance, an automotive salesperson may just look at a lost customer as simply a $500 commission lost.

However, when you calculate that customer's lifelong value, looking at the average trade cycle being 2-3 years and multiply that by the average amount of vehicles that a customer will buy over the next 20 years, that means that $500 commission turns into 8 purchases over the next 20 years, which makes that customer's value $4,000 so far...

now, multiply that times an average of 3 referrals per transaction... So that would be 8 transactions multiplied by 3 referrals which is 24 transactions...even though the commission rate usually ends up being higher on a referral for math purposes we will keep the math the same...so 24 transactions multiplied by an average $500 commission is 12,000 dollars regarding a each customers total value to you not simply a $500 one time commission.

This type of paradigm shift should alter how you look at your customers. Aside from the fact that every customer should be treated properly, this additional alteration in the thought process surrounding each customers value may be added incentive. Applying this formula could, *then change a customer's value from a simple $500 to $1,000 to, in some cases, $20,000 to $100,000 in lifetime customer value to you personally!* So that's a big reason why follow-up is important and not to be forgotten.

ALL IS FAIR IN LOVE AND SALES

Missed Sale Follow-up

Missed sale follow-up is also extremely important. Follow-up with a missed sale often happens ... as soon as a sale is missed, we will follow-up, follow-up, follow-up ... and then after a week's time or in some cases even a few days' time, that customer is considered a cold prospect and the customer ends up buying at a different place.

Follow-up with a missed sale should happen until the customer buys or dies. Even after they buy it at another place. Sometimes your product or service wasn't right at the time. Sometimes it may have been due to the lack of availability. So following up even with the people who did not purchase from you, still sending them birthday cards or gift cards or whatever your system of follow-up is can essentially convert this customer over to you because chances are, the person that they did purchase from is not going to have the rigorous follow-up that you are going to.

One of my favorite examples of this is a gentleman by the name of Charles Smith who was also an automotive sales professional. Even for the customers who did not purchase from him, he would make sure that he imputed their information his follow up system. He would simply send them the birthday cards, all of those things that were on his post sale follow-up regime. He would also send out a note that says, "Hey sorry that we were not able to do business together at this time. I still would love the opportunity to earn your business in the future. I hope that Charlise, your daughter is having a great birthday and just know that you guys are still thought about here at our dealership."

In doing this, he was able to convert a lot of people who he did not sell to initially, to being lifelong customers of his. This is how important follow-up is.

Now, when I say follow up until a customer buys or dies, this may sound harsh. This doesn't mean to pester a customer; it means to systemically follow up. Some statistics show that over 83% of sales are made between the 5th and 12th contact. Ironically, statistics also show that about 80% of sales representatives don't follow up past the 2nd contact. So, what that means is, there's a direct correlation between

ALL IS FAIR IN LOVE AND SALES

20% of the people making 80% of the money and follow-ups. I can guarantee you that it's those who follow up first, and those who continuously follow up that win the business.

When a customer doesn't buy, keep in mind that it's a marathon, not a sprint. Follow-up is the one of the most important and the final steps in the 6 steps to sales success!

ALL IS FAIR IN LOVE AND SALES

Afterword

Sales like love knows no limit and no bounds. It touches virtually every aspect of our lives in some way. For many love is necessary to function in life. Whether it be the love of a spouse, familial or the love of a friend. Sales is necessary in life also. Whether you are an entrepreneur, a leader selling his ideas to his team or on a job interview selling the hiring manager about why you should be employed.

The better that you become at mastering the art of sales, communication and persuasion the more that you can obtain out of life both secularly and personally. Love and sales go hand in hand. Both love and sales are universally understood concepts that have shaped the world that we live in today. Live, love, laugh and sell! Remember,
All is fair in love and sales!

About the Author

  Chris Singleton grew up in the small rural East, Texas towns. Center, Texas and Nacogdoches, Texas. He has endured such trials as poverty, incarceration, homelessness and becoming a teenage father while still in high school. His story is one for the ages. A story of how a small-town boy endured every trial that life handed him with grit, determination and perseverance.

  He has since gone on to own multiple companies and speak all over the country and author a book. His utmost endeavor is to simply help people achieve their goals in life. He views his life as living proof that anything is possible. Never give up on your dreams. Never let anyone tell you that you can't accomplish the things that you want to in life

His objective is that the readers of this book are not only inspired to achieve greatness, but also have tangible tools and techniques to help them get there. Keep in mind that wisdom is applied knowledge and what was contained in the afore pages contain knowledge from one of the world's leading sales experts. Now, it's up to you to go apply these tools in your life and in your business!

If you are already in sales or business and want to establish better habits of success, get better at your craft, looking to start a business or would simply like additional information regarding Chris Singleton's sales, leadership and entrepreneurship coaching program, email him directly at allisfairinloveandsales@gmail.com and book a consultation with Chris Singleton himself.